BLUE

BLUE

350 Inspiring Ways to Decorate with Blue

House Beautiful

Lisa Cregan

HEARST BOOKS
A division of Sterling Publishing Co., Inc.

New York / London
www.sterlingpublishing.com

" Put a little blue in everything you do. "
—T. KELLER DONOVAN, DESIGNER

CONTENTS

Part 1

A ROOM-BY-ROOM TOUR OF THE WORLD OF BLUE

Part 2

WHAT WORKS WITH BLUE?

Part 3

HOW BLUE ARE YOU?

INTRODUCTION

SO YOU LOVE BLUE? YOU'RE NOT ALONE.
America's had a love affair with blue ever since
Betsy Ross stitched those crisp white stars onto their
deep navy ground. Blue can be cool and restful,
swaggeringly bold, or bashfully neutral. It will
soothe the cosmopolitan swirl of a city apartment
or give a country place a dose of dazzle.

For some reason blue is also the color readers
have always associated with *House Beautiful*.
That's quite a compliment: There's no color with
more range and versatility. Interior designers
rhapsodize about the color blue the way Stephen
Stills sang about Judy Collins's eyes ("Suite: Judy
Blue Eyes"). Scattered across these pages you'll
find a compendium of designers' bluesy opinions
alongside photos of the real rooms where those
opinions became practice.

In Part 1 decorators offer their insights through
a room-by-room tour of blues for every space in

your home. Next, in Part 2 we take the mystery out of mixing blue with other colors, like white! And last, Part 3 examines how to calibrate your blues—from a lot to a little. Somewhere in here you're going to find your own "blue heaven."

Putting this book together required a deep re-reading of the delightful interviews that filled the pages of *House Beautiful* once Stephen Drucker took the reins as editor in chief in 2006 and that have continued to appear under Newell Turner's editorship. To *House Beautiful's* brilliant executive editor Barbara King and to the writers and interior designers whose lively conversations contributed so many insights, chuckles, and just sheer pleasure to *Blue*, a heartfelt "thank you." And to senior editor Christine Pittel, who provides the monthly color column, *House Beautiful's* most popular, thank you, too, for making this book's "Spectacular Blue Moments" a no-lose proposition.

—LISA CREGAN

Part 1

America's top designers and
the editors of House Beautiful
take you on a room-by-room
tour of the world of Blue.

As if it weren't
charming enough,
it's blue, too! **JOHN
PEIXINHO'S 1730**
house is painted
**Newport Blue from
California Paints.**

chapter : 1

FOYER BLUES

When you want to tell the world right up front you're seriously obsessed with blue.

ABOVE: **"The Prussian blue gives the entrance hall a great sense of arrival: It announces itself." —Jeffrey Bilhuber**

OPPOSITE: **For the entrance hall of a Pennsylvania farmhouse, Jeffrey Bilhuber chose a regal blue based on a color he'd seen while touring Mount Vernon.**

⋮ **BLUE WALLS** ⋮
MAKE AN ENTRANCE

KEITH IRVINE LIKES TO START WITH THE SHOCK OF
BENJAMIN MOORE UTAH SKY 2065-40

"It's a clean, simple jolt of blue. Simple, like all good American traditions, and I would use it in an entrance hall, against a clear white trim. It's sort of like shock tactics. Get them used to the excitement of a real color here, and then the next injection of color will be a hell of a lot easier."

. . . .

MILES REDD MIXES LODEN GREEN AND CINNAMON WITH
FINE PAINTS OF EUROPE RAL 5020

"This is a deep, deep indigo blue. There's something fluid and mysterious about the color, which is part of its allure. Picture a paintbrush dipped in India ink, and then the color it makes when you plunge it into a glass of water. I've used this in an entrance hall with loden green and cinnamon and straw."

. . . .

STEVEN GAMBREL BRINGS THE SKY INSIDE WITH PRATT &
LAMBERT ARGENT 1322

"Those great 18th-century British architects kept the front hallway somber to recall the color of the stone outside, on the façade. I like that idea of bringing the outside in, but stone doesn't necessarily work for me. I tend to use a sky-bluish color that has a pretty heavy dose of gray and green."

14

POOL PARTY
DESIGNER: RUTHIE SOMMERS
A fantastic first impression is made with watery blue walls. This astonishing swimming-pool-cool color in the foyer is Benjamin Moore Blue Seafoam.

ALEX PAPACHRISTIDIS LIKES BROWN WOOD FURNITURE WITH BENJAMIN MOORE BLUE TOILE 748

"I like aqua blues. They're both calming and refreshing, and they always look so beautiful with brown wood floors and brown wood furniture. This particular shade has the glamour and dash of a Pucci dress and would be very stylish in an entry foyer."

BARCLAY BUTERA MIXES PINK AND NAVY WITH RALPH LAUREN MYSTIC RIVER SS21

"This reminds me of one of those great English stately-home sort of blues, because it's got a touch of gray in it and they put a lot of gray in their colors. But here the gray actually makes it feel more transparent. This is a very elegant color. I can see it in an entryway with a black-and-white marble floor and touches of pink and navy."

CHARLOTTE MOSS SEES RED AND GOLD WITH BENJAMIN MOORE JAMESTOWN BLUE HC-148

"What Virginia girl wouldn't love Jamestown Blue? In certain lights, it's blue; in others, it has a haze of green. Its spectrum includes aquamarine, robin's egg, and faded Prussian blue. It's slate mixed with fog. And it's receptive to a range of partners, like Veronese gold, Chinese red, and cantaloupe."

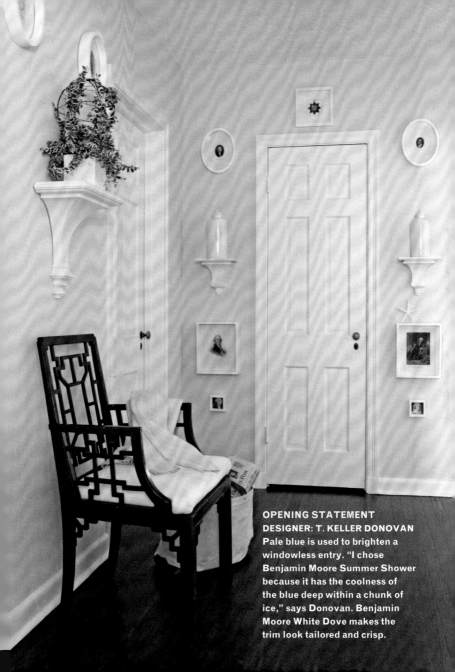

OPENING STATEMENT
DESIGNER: T. KELLER DONOVAN
Pale blue is used to brighten a windowless entry. "I chose Benjamin Moore Summer Shower because it has the coolness of the blue deep within a chunk of ice," says Donovan. Benjamin Moore White Dove makes the trim look tailored and crisp.

GREETINGS | DESIGNER: ALEX PAPACHRISTIDIS

"Whenever I see a stone floor in a foyer, I think of this place in France called Château de Groussay. There's a stone floor there with a beautiful octagonal skirted table. It softens the space," says Papachristidis. Table is skirted in Claremont Serge Antique.

WARM WELCOME
DESIGNER: T. KELLER DONOVAN
"The fabric we chose for the table says it all about this house—it's happy, warm, charming, and a little wacky," says Donovan. Walls papered in Rose Cumming Directoire Star are a stylish foil for Raoul Textiles Miranda on a skirted table.

SPECTACULAR BLUE MOMENTS

Inspired Vessels

Paris from Oly Studio

Goldfish hand-painted porcelain from Shanghai Tang

Aalto in Ultramarine by Alvar Aalto for Iittala

Blue Canton Trumpet Vase from Mottahedeh

Garden Street Rose Bowl by Kate Spade

Nuvem by Fratelli Campana for Alessi

In this Brooklyn entry by **JONATHAN BERGER** a blue and white ginger jar is a perfect accent against walls painted Benjamin Moore's Razzle Dazzle.

SPECTACULAR BLUE MOMENTS

Underfoot

Mandala Denim cotton flatweave from Madeline Weinrib

Paisley in Aqua from Merida Meridian

Indo Gabbeh from Ikea

French Check in Blue Check from Karastan

Concentric Squares in Sky from Company C

Marrakesh from The Conran Shop

A soaring entry hall by **DIAMOND BARATTA** is brought down to earth with a custom-made blue rug.

chapter : 2

LIVING ROOM BLUES

When you want to spend every living
moment in blue.

ABOVE: "We debated about giving more color to the walls—something with a
bit more blue in it—but I think we're happy that we left it. There's plenty of blue
going on." —Meg Braff.

OPPOSITE: Braff used soft blues and whites, linens, cottons, and a seagrass
rug to forge a light, relaxed atmosphere. Walls and trim are painted Benjamin
Moore White Dove.

JAMIE DRAKE DECOMPRESSES INSIDE BENJAMIN MOORE WHITE SATIN 2067-70

"It's an *ahhhhhhhh* color, a pale, ethereal blue with a touch of periwinkle. Completely uplifting—like floating on a cloud. As soon as you walk in, you feel the weight of the world is lifted from your shoulders."

JOHN GILMER IS CRAZY ABOUT LACQUERING OVER RALPH LAUREN BALTIC BLUE IB86

"This is a true peacock blue, the blue of David Hockney's California swimming pools. It reminds me of those endless, carefree summers as a child. It's a happy blue, beautiful and soothing during the day, but at night it comes alive, wrapping you in its warm, velvety embrace. Lacquer it to bring out the depth of the color."

MARY DOUGLAS DRYSDALE LOVES HIGH HEELS AND BENJAMIN MOORE JAMAICAN AQUA 2048-60

"This is a pale teal, a really lovely neoclassical color that goes with high heels and beautiful earrings. But it's also sassy and romantic. It reminds me of sitting on the beach someplace and having that wonderful waiter come up and say, 'Now, what would you like?'"

ALL BOOKED UP
DESIGNER: KRISTEN PANITCH
Dark gray-blue on the walls and bookshelves—Farrow & Ball Down Pipe 26—creates a cozy yet sophisticated room.

JOHN YUNI SEES BOTTLE-GREEN VELVET UPHOLSTERY WITH BENJAMIN MOORE AQUARIUS 788

"I've never met a blue I didn't like. Everything from the darkest to the lightest—and this is in the middle with a hint of aquamarine. A blue living room would be glamorous, especially with bottle-green silk velvet upholstery and a touch of silver or gold on a chair. And walls should be slick, for sparkle. It can never be too glossy for me."

MILES REDD'S STARS ALIGN WITH BENJAMIN MOORE CARIBBEAN BLUE WATER 2055-30

"I'm a Pisces, so I generally find myself swimming in a sea of blue. I love rainy days. I love water. This is a color you see in Chinese porcelain, Marie Antoinette's Versailles, and Picasso's blue period—cool and hard, yet at the same time warm and enveloping. I think it goes with everything, but then again I believe all colors go together."

THOMAS JAYNE GOES OLD WORLD WITH BENJAMIN MOORE HEAVENLY BLUE 709

"This is the color of the sky in Old Master paintings, when the varnish has yellowed. It has a luminous quality. You could paint the whole room or just the floor—you'd feel as if you were floating."

STRIPES ARE STARS
DESIGNER: MEG BRAFF
Blue striped wallpaper and
trim painted Farrow & Ball
Stone Blue 86 lend these
walls mysterious depth.

A BLUE LAGOON

DESIGNER MILLY DE CABROL

"It's a soft gray-blue on these walls, a warm Mediterranean blue—Benjamin Moore Yarmouth Blue HC-150—like the watery blues you see in Venice."

"I asked the painters to do a subtle strié, so you see little streaks of dark and light. That's the way it would be in a Venetian palazzo."

"Isn't it interesting how one object like that blue ostrich feather pillow from Dransfield & Ross can make a living room feel so young?"

SUMMERY
DESIGNER: DAVID LAWRENCE
A blue sofa covered in Vizir in Indigo from Old World Weavers topped with Ralph Lauren throw pillows makes for the perfect summery living room. Walls are Benjamin Moore Super White.

HIGH SPIRITS | DESIGNER: CARLETON VARNEY
"It has an air of happiness," says Varney, about a sofa dressed in Potalla by China Seas and walls painted Farrow & Ball Cook's Blue 237.

PIZZAZZ

DESIGNER JONATHAN ADLER

"Color is a great way to express playfulness. Throughout the house, we used turquoise, yellow, lime green, black and white, with nothing toned down."

"We went with a programmatic approach—the black and white foundation with a splash of turquoise."

"We painted all the floors white, which is something I always love to do for instant happiness."

Black, white, and turquoise make a graphic splash in fashion designer Liz Lange's house. The statement-making ottoman is upholstered in Hinson's Montauk Texture in Aegean.

Elsie de Wolfe

SPECTACULAR BLUE MOMENTS

Punctuation

Blue Larch Pinecone from Agnes & Hoss

Charcoal Suzani from Anthropologie

Z Gallerie's Circa Pillow in Azure.

Gilded Beetle from Ige Design

Teal Printed Metallic from John Robshaw

Gramercy Sea from Michael Devine

Peacock from Home Boutique of Greenwich

ALLISON CACCOMA covers pillows in Cowtan & Tout Mongiardino Celedon and Manuel Canovas Polidoro Van Loo silk velvet on a sofa dressed in Manuel Canovas Savannah Ecru.

DIVAS | DESIGNER: DIAMOND BARATTA

Taking cues from 20th-century art and fashion, Diamond Baratta designed a rug
inspired by a Josef Albers painting, and windowpane-check fabric for upholstery
echoing a vintage Balenciaga coat.

BEACHY | DESIGNER: ANNIE SELKE
A traditional beach house gets shots of modern shapes and bright color. Curtains
are Shalini Bluemarine from Calico Corners. Rug is Fisher Ticking from Dash &
Albert. Walls are Crystal Blue 2051-70 by Benjamin Moore.

THE SIMPLE LIFE
....
DESIGNER LYNN MORGAN

"It's so comforting to see blues and greens everywhere. It creates such serenity and warmth."

"Creamy walls with glossy white trim always help rooms to breathe naturally."

Sofas covered in Summer Cloth in Seaspray, and club chairs in China Seas' Hawthorne, are soft and understated. But the zebra print, Grammont Linen by Travers, is a jolt of high-impact glamour.

SPECTACULAR BLUE MOMENTS

Party Tables

Blue damask glass-topped
table from Worlds Away

Iris End Table from
Rowe Fine Furniture

Vintage-looking dhurrie-
covered English trunks
from Guinevere Antiques

Marbella Buffet from
SHINE by S.H.O.

The enormous deep blue coffee table designed by
TOM STRINGER has star appeal, especially when used
to store stacks of bright yellow *National Geographics*.

A BLUE SOFA
GIVES A LIVING ROOM A DEEP-SEATED PUNCH

TODD ROMANO WRAPS UP IN ROCHELLE IN AQUA FROM NORTHCROFT

"Durable, beautiful. The chicest apartment I've ever been to had this velvet everywhere."

KATIE RIDDER LOVES FLAMINIA IN AZURE FROM MARVIC

"Flaminia is a workhorse fabric. It's linen, viscose, and polyester. The viscose makes it crisp, which is so ideal for tight upholstery."

MICHAEL WHALEY FAVORS ROSS IN BLUE FROM JANE CHURCHILL

"Looks like the sea—so pretty and restful. Plus it's soft, cozy, and a great background for pillows."

ANTONIA HUTT IS CRAZY ABOUT PRIMA ALPACA IN PARCELA FROM SANDRA JORDAN

"If I could, I'd cover everything in my house in Prima Alpaca. It's the most gorgeous and luxurious fabric I've ever seen. Even the color is luxurious."

THOMAS O'BRIEN RECOMMENDS GROUNDWORKS TAMORA WEAVE IN AEGEAN

"A really good-textured woven in a chic pattern that works on any kind of chair."

BLUE NOTES | DESIGNER: JOE NAHEM

Blue velvet sofas lend a room uncommon ground. Back-to-back sofas, upholstered in Marlowe in India Ink, have "an iridescent quality," Nahem says. "The color changes depending on the light. One day it's gray, another day it's blue."

CRISP | DESIGNER: T. KELLER DONOVAN

"There are these wonderful Palladian windows in the living room, and I decided to draw attention to them with a long banquette," says Donovan. Pierre Frey's Colorado fabric in Admiral Blue covers the sofa.

ROMANTIC | DESIGNER: ANNE MILLER

"Once I got the blue walls up I thought there wasn't enough contrast, so I did white curtains with silver-leaf hardware against them," says Miller. Walls are custom hand-painted de Gournay panels.

BLUE CURTAINS
SET THE STAGE

TODD ROMANO FRAMES WINDOWS IN FIORELLA IN VAN DYKE FROM ROGERS & GOFFIGON

"What a delicious color. It's the palest aqua with an almost imperceptible strié."

PETER DUNHAM SUGGESTS KASHMIR PAISLEY FROM PETER DUNHAM TEXTILES

"I call it a 'go-everywhere' print, because it mixes with almost anything."

ANTONIA HUTT LOVES PIZZELLE IN BABY BLUE FROM GALBRAITH & PAUL

"It's stiff, but I like that look. And I'd also paint my walls the same color turquoise—the curtains become one with the room."

SCOTT SALVATOR PICKS VICEROY STRIE IN CANTON BLUE FROM BRUNSCHWIG & FILS

"It's easy to use. Its geometric modern look works for curtains."

JOE NYE LINES THEM IN VANESSA'S FOLLY IN TURQUOISE FROM BRUNSCHWIG & FILS

"I use this all the time to line curtains. I'd do pillows with it, too. Repetition is good—it ties a room together."

LONG LINES
DESIGNER: CHRISTOPHER MAYA
Grandly arched windows in an
18-foot-high living room are framed
by the icy blue of Holland & Sherry
Glace curtains in Glacier.

chapter 3

DINING ROOM BLUES

When you want blue as your centerpiece.

ABOVE: **In a new house, designer Joe Nahem gave the dining room timeless allure with a hand-painted and embroidered silk wallcovering, Fromental's Lotus and Carp in Moon Gold, paired with deep blue moldings and trim.**

OPPOSITE: **"The room is so big and gets so much light, we thought it would make it feel a little cozier to paint the wainscot and trim a dark blue." —Joe Nahem.**

WHITNEY STEWART IS EMPHATIC ABOUT C2, ELECTRIC 275

"Forget all those pale shades. What you want is an evening blue, an Yves Klein blue. Deeper than deep. You see it on Byzantine ceilings, in Jean Paul Gaultier's stripes. It's contemplative, meditative, mysterious. When I want to be enveloped, blue is the only color that will do it for me."

BARCLAY BUTERA MAKES A NOBLE GESTURE WITH RALPH LAUREN CALYPSO VM138

"It's a blue with a certain nobility, something you would have seen in a colonial house in Williamsburg. But it's also a casual and comfortable color. A dining room should be approachable—don't think it's only for holidays and special events."

MARK EPSTEIN SILHOUETTES THE TABLE AGAINST BENJAMIN MOORE PHILIPSBURG BLUE HC-159

"In a dining room in a 1960s building one wall was flanked by columns and a ceiling soffit, which created a kind of frame. So I painted just that wall recess in this muted blue-gray, which has that sense of calm I look for in colors. The blue gave me a beautiful silhouette for the dark wood of the dining table."

MORE IS MORE
DESIGNER: ERIC LYSDAHL
Walls and ceiling in Benjamin
Moore Newburyport Blue
HC-155 allow the white elements
to pop while creating a rich
background for gilded sconces
and mirror frames.

A MAN'S WORLD | DESIGNER: MARY McDONALD'S

Blue walls for this bachelor client are painted Sherwin-Williams Frank Blue 6967—a conservative masculine color that's sexy in this context. The diamond weave rug is from **Dash & Albert**.

54

: BLUE WALLS :

BACKDROPS YOU'LL DISH ABOUT

CARL D'AQUINO DEEPENS A DARK ROOM WITH BENJAMIN
MOORE GULF STREAM 670

"I've always loved north light. Without the direct
sun, it's more constant and uniform, which is
why artists love to work in a north-facing studio.
This rich blue-green becomes even deeper in
north light. We did it 18th-century style in a
dining room—painting out all the moldings and
baseboards instead of highlighting them."

PHILIP NIMMO PAINTS ONE WALL BENJAMIN MOORE
DARK ROYAL BLUE 2065-20

"I did a dining room with three dove-gray walls and
one dark blue wall, a royal blue with just a little,
little bit of red in it. At night, with the shine from
the silver on the table, it was sexy, sexy, sexy—
without consuming the room. It looked fathomless."

CAROLYNE ROEHM LIKES TO SEE CORAL OR ROSE WITH
FARROW & BALL LIGHT BLUE 22

"God knows, I love blue, and I love Farrow &
Ball's blues because they always have that little
thing that's different. This has a greenish cast,
which warms it up and keeps it from being too
sweet. That's why it looks so beautiful with pink,
rose, coral, and red."

MODERNISM

DESIGNER KELLY VAN PATTER

"Anything I put in this room took on a blue color because of the reflections from my swimming pool. So I thought, 'I just need to roll with the blue and come up with a color that works.'"

"I'm not a person who likes blue a lot, but this is a steely grayish-blue— Benjamin Moore Nocturnal Gray— and I wanted to stay with an industrial palette without being too cold."

This room is a tribute to interior designer Kelly Van Patter's first career as a TV production designer: table and bench are mementoes from *The Apprentice*; the ostrich eggs and bowl were props on *Survivor*.

CHINOISERIE | DESIGNER: SALLY SWING

"I've always loved chinoiserie. About ten years ago, my sister visited Sweden and brought back a book with pictures of the Chinese Pavilion at Drottningholm Palace, which is filled with 18th-century chinoiserie. This is my own Chinese pavilion, my fantasy," says Swing.

SHIMMER
DESIGNER: ALLISON CACCOMA
In this dining room blue Venetian plaster walls have a waxy shine that creates a sense of motion when the light reflects off them at night.

SPECTACULAR BLUE MOMENTS

Showstoppers

**Tablestories by
Tord Boontje
through Artecnica**

**Virginia Blue
from Mottahedeh**

**Crab from Pearl
River Mart**

**Indigo from
Z Gallerie**

**Azul by Oscar
de la Renta**

**Rope in Blue from
Williams Sonoma Home**

**Heirloom
from Vietri**

Prunus from Burleigh

**Nature Collection
from Tiffany & Co.**

"Blue and white against a white painted background is always very powerful. The white plates anchor the four corners. They create a plus sign that gives a kind of visual motion to everything. If the corners were anchored by blue plates, it would feel more static," says **TOM STRINGER**.

LUMINOUS | DESIGNER: MARSHALL WATSON

Watson used a Duralee stripe horizontally on the chair backs, then covered the seats in a Hinson solid to calm down the pattern. To give the blue-gray wall glaze the feel of morning mist, walls were flogged with a feather duster.

CANTONESE
DESIGNER: ANNIE SELKE
Blue-and-white Canton
porcelain inspired Annie
Selke to commission the dining
room's mural. Chairs covered
in Scramble in Slate from
Calico Corners rest on a
Dash & Albert Bluemarine
ticking rug.

"There are pools of light everywhere here. We used different materials on the shades so they would give off different types of light."
—HARRY HEISSMANN

ALL THE TRIMMINGS

DESIGNERS ALBERT HADLEY
AND HARRY HEISSMANN

Antique dining chairs are covered in custom-colored blue leather by Falotico Studio and accented with nailheads on red grosgrain ribbon trim. Custom blue-lacquered lampshades are lined in gold.

"I realized the chairs had an amazing shape. The clients wanted fabric that was suitable for a dining room, so we chose blue leather because of the blue stripe in the curtains." — **HARRY HEISSMANN**

A CHAMELEON | DESIGNER: KRISTEN PANITCH

"The wall color in the dining room is the ultimate chameleon blue," says
Panitch. "It's lighter in the morning, and then toward evening it deepens and
feels moodier." Walls are painted Farrow & Ball Blackened 2011 and chairs are
slipcovered in Jasper's Indian Flower in Blue.

"I use these comfortable dining chairs over
and over again," says Hodgins. Rose Tarlow
chairs are covered in Aquitaine in Slate
from Scalamandré.

SPORTY

DESIGNER DIAMOND BARATTA

"In the last few years people are asking for much more contemporary. I think a lot of people all of a sudden said yikes, we're in the 21st century, let's start living like it."

Diamond Baratta
designed the director's
chairs based on a
classic Jean-Michel
Frank design, with
child-friendly blue
leather seats.

chapter : 4

KITCHEN BLUES

When you want your kitchen to be the
happy blue hub of the house.

ABOVE: **Benjamin Moore Polo Blue 2062-10 creates drama and mystery in Windsor
Smith's kitchen, yet doesn't feel heavy because it's set off with a Thassos marble
tile floor.**

OPPOSITE: **"I started out with navy but that felt too nautical and I kept going darker
until I got to this color you can't quite define." —Windsor Smith**

CLARE DONOHUE USES BENJAMIN MOORE WEDGEWOOD GRAY HC-146 ON WALLS, WITH WOODLAWN BLUE HC-147 ON THE CEILING

"Wedgewood Gray and Woodlawn Blue have that robin's egg vibe. I always hedge my bets toward grayed-down shades, because bright colors that look so happy in the paint store can look bizarre in real life. If you're nervous, start by painting the back wall inside the cabinets."

SUSAN ZISES GREEN SEES LIME GREEN AND WHITE WITH BENJAMIN MOORE HOUSE OF BLUES 758

"This reminds me of a Tiffany box, and what's better than Tiffany? It's like a clear summer sky with a tinge of twilight on the horizon. Bring in pink, lime green. White, to keep it fresh. I used it in a kitchen and it really opened it up. It's a boundless color."

T. KELLER DONOVAN'S OWN KITCHEN IS PAINTED BENJAMIN MOORE STUNNING 826

"The colors I like are very pure and uncomplicated. This is a nice, regular, all-American, patriotic, down-to-earth blue, with no weird tones in it. It's a happy blue. I used it in my kitchen, where it's a great background for all my antique Spode china—traditional, but still young, fun, and fresh."

CHARM SCHOOL | DESIGNER: ANNIE SELKE
The walls of this beach house's kitchen are painted a sunny blue, Glidden Shimmering Sky, to offset green-stripe chairs and a table from Annie Selke Home.

BOTTOM LINES | DESIGNER: TOBI FAIRLEY
Floor stripes in **Wythe Blue** by Benjamin Moore and **Wool Skein** by Sherwin-Williams mix well with **Oly's Ajax** side chairs covered in **Highland Court Palazzo** in **Aqua** and **Cocoa**.

: BLUE FLOORS :
PUT A SHINE ON A KITCHEN

GARY McBOURNIE FRESHENS AN OLD FLOOR WITH
BENJAMIN MOORE DEEP OCEAN 2058-30

"Blue was a natural for a Nantucket boathouse
kitchen floor, and it brightened all that old wood.
Then we spattered it with red, white, and blue, so
you don't notice all the sand you track in. You just
tap a wet paintbrush against a strip of wood, but
it's more difficult to control than you'd think."

EMILY HENRY GETS THE SANTA FE LOOK WITH BENJAMIN
MOORE SPECTRA BLUE 2049-50

"Why not put the sky on the floor? Sooo cool. It's
unexpected, contemporary, upside down! This
turquoise is the color of our Santa Fe sky on a
clear day. Hang an antler chandelier and you've
got a hip, affordable Santa Fe look."

STEVEN SCLAROFF PAINTS BENJAMIN MOORE GRAY OWL
2137-60 OVER BENJAMIN MOORE BLUE JEAN 2062-50

"I just painted a floor in two colors, a gray khaki
over a dirtied-up sky blue, so as you walk over it
the blue starts to show through. It creates this nice
scruffy look, as if it has aged over a long time —
but it happens faster. When you reach that ideal
moment and it looks pleasantly worn, finish it
with clear polyurethane to preserve it."

AQUARIUS | DESIGNER: FRANK ROOP

The star of this kitchen is the blue tile backsplash of variegated handmade glass tiles that's so reminiscent of the ocean. Tile is by Erin Adams through Ann Sacks. The countertops are jet-mist granite, and a bleached drift-oak island is custom-colored a driftwood gray-blue.

SPECTACULAR BLUE MOMENTS

Set the Scene

Dutch Faux-Tile wallpaper From Warner

Contour in Mosaic sculptured vinyl paper from Graham & Brown

Potager in Robins Egg vinyl-backed paper from Brunschwig & Fils

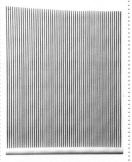

Beckley Stripe in Navy on White vinyl-coated paper from Hinson & Company

Xiang Suay in Blue matte vinyl paper from China Seas through Quadrille

In a kitchen by **ERIN MARTIN** a blue and white painted design brings walls, and even the barrel-vaulted ceiling, to life. "It's suggestive of blue and white china, which is perfect for a kitchen," says Martin.

OFF THE DEEP END

ARCHITECT KATHRYN FEE
DESIGNER BARBARA UZIELLI

"The bold color adds a bit of an edge to a traditional kitchen."
—KATHRYN FEE

White Carrara marble countertops, finished with a traditional ogee edge, set off cabinets painted Benjamin Moore Champion Cobalt.

"There's so much light that the color never gets too dark, even on a gloomy day. It's a deep cobalt blue that we pulled out of a piece of Chinese porcelain."
—Homeowner
LISA McCARTHY

EXOTIC | DESIGNER: ERIN MARTIN

"The tiles are an inspirational shade of blue. They're French, but they remind me of Morocco," says Martin, about the blue and white backsplash tiles from Country Floors.

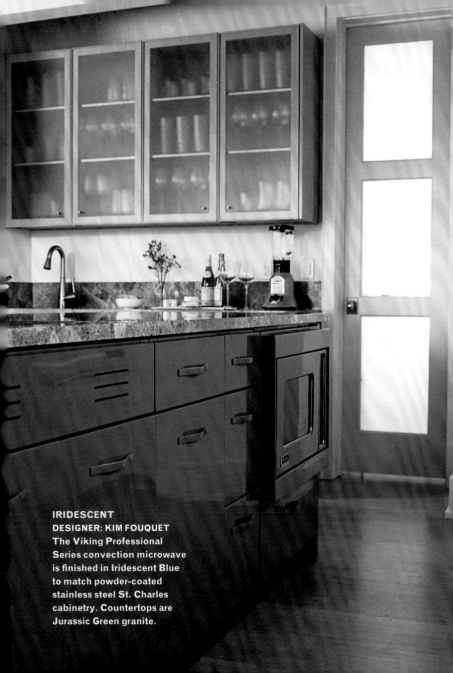

IRIDESCENT
DESIGNER: KIM FOUQUET
The Viking Professional Series convection microwave is finished in Iridescent Blue to match powder-coated stainless steel St. Charles cabinetry. Countertops are Jurassic Green granite.

BREEZY

DESIGNER: ASHLEY WHITTAKER
The blue and white cotton dhurry
from Stark breaks up a large
expanse of floor. Walls are in Linen
White and trim is Ivory White,
both Benjamin Moore.

FLIRTY | DESIGNER: JONATHAN BERGER
French chairs from the 1940s are covered in blue leather with pink-dyed cowhide backs from Global Leathers. And Berger created a big, whimsical bulletin board out of plaster and pale-blue-painted cork.

COMFORT ZONE | DESIGNER: SCOTT SANDERS

A wide-open white kitchen is made warm and comfy thanks to lots of navy and
chocolate brown striped upholstery.

PRACTICAL MAGIC | DESIGNER: MARKHAM ROBERTS

Fabric follows function—a tough-as-nails blue cotton strié, Chiltern by Cowtan &
Tout, covers a kitchen banquette.

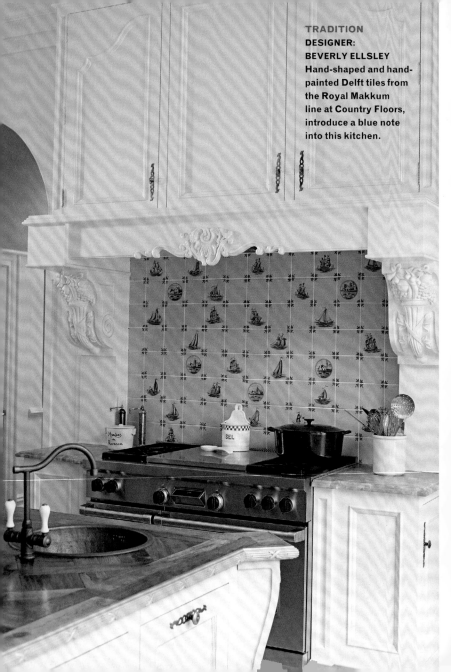

HIGH STYLE | DESIGNER: TOM SCHEERER
Made-to-order kitchen tiles from Cuban Tropical Tiles in Miami are a bit of
sunny-side-up cheerfulness. Cabinet interiors are Benjamin Moore Bird's Egg.

chapter : 5

FAMILY ROOM BLUES

When you want your family swaddled safely in blue.

LEFT: **"The clients wanted to be traditional, but still young and fresh. Fabrics had to be durable enough not to feel hands-off, or paws-off, for kids and pets."**
—Joe Nahem.

OPPOSITE: **Curtains in a bold fabric—Crewel Embroidery in Green by Decorators Walk—help ground the family room's double-height ceiling, and a custom blue sofa is upholstered in Patelin by Designtex.**

BLUE WALLS

KEEP A FAMILY SNUG

ROBIN BELL LIKES MARIGOLD AND PUCE WITH BENJAMIN
MOORE PADDINGTON BLUE 791

"This is a peacock blue, a very happy, exuberant
blue that would set off all the objects in a room.
I'd use it in a high-gloss finish with lots of white
moldings, and maybe pull in marigold or puce.
Blue is one of the best colors around for crispness
and contrast. After all, what looks better than a
naval officer in his dress blues?"

CAROLYNE ROEHM CONJURES CLOUDS WITH FARROW &
BALL PARMA GRAY 27

"Think blue skies with fluffy white clouds,
Dorothy's gingham dress in *The Wizard of Oz*.
Parma Gray is a subtle, sophisticated blue, best in
a matte finish with white trim and accents."

KRIM DANZINGER EXPANDS A SMALL SPACE WITH
GLIDDEN CLEAR BLUE SKY GLB15

"This is a clean, clear blue that suggests sky and
air and a new kind of energy. It feels pure and
trustworthy. The color doesn't come at you—it
recedes, which gives a room a nice sensation
of openness."

SURF'S UP | DESIGNER: ANNIE SELKE
Walls in this family room, painted Glidden Shimmering Sky, complement the rug, Staffordshire Stripe by Dash & Albert, and a chair covered in Bala Ticking from Annie Selke at Calico Corners.

ERIC COHLER SEES BROWN AND CAMEL AGAINST FARROW & BALL CHINESE BLUE 90

"This is not too hot, not too cold, with a lot of green, which makes it feel grounded. Blue is so regenerative. There's the idea of water, renewal. It's powerful, regal—think of blue bloods, blue ribbons. And it looks great with most other colors, especially browns and camels and beiges."

JOHN SALADINO GETS EMOTIONAL ABOUT BENJAMIN MOORE ORIENTAL IRIS 1418

"I'm attracted to periwinkle blue. It's soothing and serene and metamorphic because it goes from gray into blue into lavender, depending on the time of day, the season, and the person looking at it. No two people see color the same way. Blue combines two things I love, the ocean and the sky, which lifts me out of the quagmire of reality."

KATHRYN M. IRELAND GETS BACK TO BASICS WITH FARROW & BALL PALE POWDER #204

"I grew up on the southwest coast of Scotland, and the sea was almost this color—a gray blue with green undertones. It's a very easy color to throw things into, a good background for fabrics in pink, orange, taupe, or mustard yellow."

MOODY BLUES | DESIGNER: JOHN BARMAN

"I used this deep Mediterranean blue all over this room— on the walls, on the molding, on the cabinets, even on the floor, with a carpet in the same tone. You're swept away by the blue," says Barman. Walls are painted Fine Paints of Europe Delft Blue.

95

HOME RUN | DESIGNER: JASON BELL

In this star-studded beach-house family room, the sofa and ottoman, in Bowie in Midnight from **Norbar**, along with a compass pillow from **Lynnens**, establish a nautical tone. Armchair is covered in Chrysanthe from **Osborne & Little**.

SPONGEWARE | STYLE DESIGNER: JAMES RADIN
Benjamin Moore White Dove sets off the owners' collection of 19th-century
American spongeware. An easy chair, covered in Morelia in Robin's Egg from
Raoul Textiles, complements the pottery collection.

SUZANNE LOVELL LOVES SALISBURY STRIPE IN LAKE FROM TWILL TEXTILES

"Stripes cross all styles. Layer them by changing the scale, and make a room taller or longer by running them vertically or horizontally."

ALESSANDRA BRANCA PICKS ASPEN IN BLEU ANCIEN FROM PIERRE FREY

"It's a fun fabric. Put it on a sofa for a playful shot of color."

AMANDA NISBET GOES HORIZONTAL WITH CATWALK IN OCEAN BY LULU DK

"I'm not trying to diss the vertical, but a horizontal stripe is always more interesting."

LARRY LASLO SUGGESTS MOBY DICK IN MOODY BLUES FROM JOHN HUTTON

"I always look to a small-scale stripe like this for relief from larger patterns."

PERFECTLY ALIGNED
DESIGNER: MICHAEL SMITH
In this English country style
family room, the sofa,
covered in Jasper's Mali
Stripe in Blue, feels like
a neutral amid all the
other patterns.

DEEP COMFORT

DESIGNER ALESSANDRA BRANCA

The sofa was upholstered in **Le Gracieux's Regello** in **Bay on Soft Blue**—but first the fabric's outline's were quilted for extra coziness and durability. The carpet is from **Shyam Ahuja** and curtains are **Chelsea Editions' Stripe.**

"I love the bookcase filled with Chinese porcelains and crackled modern porcelains, set against geometrically patterned grasscloth walls."

SPECTACULAR BLUE MOMENTS

Fancy Footwork

Fancy Garden in Pearl and Sky by Michael Smith through Mansour Modern

Toile in Chocolate and Royal, Kerry Joyce for Mansour Modern

Flock in Dove/Cream by Thomas Paul through Pillows and Throws

Cloud Oushak in Water from Otegard

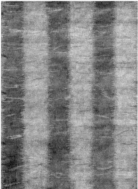

Ikat in Blue by Kathryn M. Ireland through Elson & Company

Mr. Dacery from the Stark Modern Signature Collection through Stark Carpet

HEALING BARSANTI uses a blue striped rug to break up expanses of solid upholstery.

POP ART

DESIGNER: STEVEN GAMBREL

"In this room you have a **Pop Art** version of nature— a copper green hitting a true blue."

Green walls are painted **Benjamin Moore Cedar Green** and bookshelves' interiors are in **Benjamin Moore Marlboro Blue**. The sofa is covered horizontally in **John Robshaw's Gent's Stripe**.

chapter : 6

LIBRARY BLUES

When you want a room that reads only blue.

LEFT: **"How many forgettable paneled libraries have you seen? Yet here, with nothing but a bucket of paint and a genius color, we were able to make a memorable room"** —Rob Southern

OPPOSITE: **High-gloss walls have many coats of Benjamin Moore Bermuda Turquoise, "a perfectly finessed balance of green and blue,"** says Southern. **His club chairs are covered in the boldest ikat he could find: Lee Jofa's Sokoto in Red. The curtain fabric is Giza in Red by Lee Jofa.**

MARIO BUATTA BRINGS IN REDS AND GREENS WITH
BENJAMIN MOORE BAINBRIDGE BLUE 749

"I'm blue, I'm blue! I'm a happy guy but I have
always loved blue, in all its shapes and sizes. For
libraries, I like this deep Mediterranean blue. I'd
use it glazed and shiny. Every color looks fresh
against blue. Put lemon yellow with it and it will
look like a Matisse painting."

JAN SHOWERS CREATES AFTER-HOURS GLAM WITH
BENJAMIN MOORE HALE NAVY HC-154

"I recently did a midnight blue library that is so wonderful and seductive at night. The curtains match
the walls, and the ceiling is midnight blue as well.
We used a pair of pond-green leather Louis XV–style
chairs, and they make you feel as though you might be
outdoors on a dark night with some fabulous fauna."

ROGER DE CABROL SEES '40S FURNITURE WITH BENJAMIN
MOORE PATRIOT BLUE 2064

"I don't like baby blue or sky blue—I like dark,
strong cobalt blue. It reminds me of Europe,
in the sense of luxuriousness and the privacy it
creates in a room. It shields you. I'd use it in a
study or library, and then snap it up with furniture
from the '40s or '50s and a faux-zebra rug."

BRIGHT STAR | DESIGNER: KEITH IRVINE

In Rex Harrison's library, Irvine put a coat of varnish over the blue—Benjamin Moore Dark Royal Blue 2065-20—so "you can almost see yourself reflected in it." The ceiling was glazed in a custom off-white with a touch of gold to pick up the glint of Harrison's many awards.

DOUBLE VISION | DESIGNER: SCOTT SANDERS

"A soft, soothing blue is an unexpected choice in a library. I didn't want to paint the moldings the usual black or white but still needed a nice contrast, and came up with chocolate brown." Walls are painted Farrow & Ball Parma Gray and trim is in Mahogany 36.

110

A LINE DRAWING | **DESIGNER: ROBIN BELL**

Walls upholstered in a cozy Peter Fasano blue-and-green stripe bring the
formality of a high ceiling and intricate moldings down a notch.

SPECTACULAR BLUE MOMENTS

Command Posts

**Writing desk from
Russell & Mackenna**

**Randall Club in Light Blue
from Williams Sonoma Home**

**Rita in Kipling Sky Blue from
Lulu DK for Elite Leather**

**Rokoko from Country
Swedish**

CELERIE KEMBLE says always be bold: She used a
striking blue leather wing chair from Brunschwig & Fils
to fill this office space.

SMART | DESIGNER: BETSY BURNHAM
A blue Chinese Chippendale armchair from Jonathan Adler and a swath of Travers zebra print in blue make a chic spot to park a computer.

DESIGNER: T. KELLER DONOVAN
Donovan's rule is that whenever
he does a blue and white room it
has to have the punch of natural
tones, like the faux-wood wallpaper from **Nobilis** in this library.

SPECTACULAR BLUE MOMENTS

Brilliance

Batik Blue & White from Arteriors Home

Christina in Turquoise from Bungalow 5

Go Cha table lamp from Jamie Young

Willow Blue with Diamente Shade from Worlds Away

Palecek's Blue Reef resin table lamp

Since a mahogany-paneled library tends to be dark, **MARKHAM ROBERTS** says, "almost everything was chosen for its ability to pop," including the 1920s blue glass vases mounted as lamps.

chapter : 7

BEDROOM BLUES

When you want to sleep in a sea of blue.

ABOVE: **"I took four grommeted navy-blue curtain panels. Then I got some curtain hardware from Restoration Hardware and just stuck it in the ceiling. It's a no-muss, no-fuss four-poster bed, and it creates an instant sense of grandeur. But it's a *cheeky* grandeur." —Jonathan Adler**

OPPOSITE: **Jonathan Adler's Joy Needlepoint pillow rests against two of his Bargello Flame pillows.**

MICHAEL SIMON SOOTHES WITH SHERWIN WILLIAMS TOPSAIL SW6217

"I can't say it's aqua and I can't say it's gray. It's in the space between those colors. It's a very pale blue, and blue is a color that evokes calm. When the clouds clear and the sky displays its depths, or water reflects and distorts the sky, it reveals shades and hues that defy description but are deeply felt. Blue transports you inward to a contemplative state."

MALLORY MARSHALL SEES SHADES OF PARIS IN MURALO PAINTS DAYDREAM P380

"I was looking for a color that was as honest as E.B. White and as inspiring as Carl Sandburg. I went through many that were too strong or too insipid, too feminine or too masculine. This is the color of a deep breath in early spring, a true gray-blue, like the gutters in Paris."

CLODAGH MIXES BURNISHED METALLICS WITH BENJAMIN MOORE MIDNIGHT NAVY 2067-10

"Ask any man what his favorite color is and he'll probably say blue. It's a thoughtful color. There's a mystery to deep, deep indigo blue. It's calming. Beautiful in a bedroom—it helps promote sleep. I love it with golds and burnished metallics. It's limitless."

DREAM TEAM
DESIGNER: ERIC COHLER
Walls upholstered in Holland & Sherry's Glacier offset a headboard covered in Lee Jofa's Lela Embroidery in Cocoa.

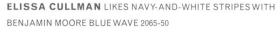

ELISSA CULLMAN LIKES NAVY-AND-WHITE STRIPES WITH BENJAMIN MOORE BLUE WAVE 2065-50

"Blue is tricky. It can go gray and sad. But not this warm Mediterranean blue. It's the blue in all those Pucci prints, a bright, happy, not-a-cloud-in-the-sky blue, as if you're in vacation mode and having lobster and rosé at Tetou, on the beach near Cannes. I love it in a bedroom, where you could crisp it up with a navy-and-white striped fabric and one of those great Elizabeth Eakins plaid rugs."

MILES REDD'S OWN BEDROOM IS PAINTED BENJAMIN MOORE BIRD'S EGG 2051- 60

"I go towards cool and airy in the bedroom. That to me seems restful, sleep inducing. My own particular bedroom is painted pale blue, with touches of silver gray and coral. I'm a Pisces and I'm always gravitating to water and cool colors."

PHOEBE HOWARD DREAMS OF BENJAMIN MOORE GLASS SLIPPER 1632

"I've used this color so much that the paint chip is all bent and splattered with marks, as in a cookbook. When I was five years old, I made my mother paint my room this color—a pale sky blue with a little gray in it. It's strong and fragile at the same time."

MATCH POINT | DESIGNER: PHOEBE HOWARD
Howard demonstrates her love for walls painted Benjamin Moore Glass Slipper,
even matching curtains to its blue-gray hue.

YIN AND YANG | **DESIGNER: MARKHAM ROBERTS**

Roberts balanced masculine and feminine with blues, teals, and browns:
"We wanted the room to be comfortable for both men and women," says Roberts.
Curtain rods are painted to look like bamboo. **Headboard fabric is Khan Cashmere
from Holland & Sherry. Curtain fabric is Lore from Robert Allen.**

124

PALATIAL | **DESIGNER: BUNNY WILLIAMS**
A dazzling custom mirrored bed—dressed in
Pratesi sheets—reflects all the blue-gray hues
of the embroidered Indian wall hanging behind
it. The silvery carpet was found at Beauvais.

HIGH GLAM

DESIGNER: SUZANNE KASLER
Walls painted ICI/Glidden Westerly
Wind up the feminine quotient in
this glam room. The four-poster bed
from Louis J. Solomon is reflected in
mirrored nightstands from Horchow
and an antique painted white bench
is upholstered in Villemont Stripe,
from Travis & Company.

NIGHT LIGHT | **DESIGNER: ALLISON CACCOMA**

"The owners fell in love with this floral fabric, and the wonderful surprise of high-gloss paint on the walls highlights it so beautifully," says Caccoma. Walls are high gloss—Benjamin Moore Harbor Haze 2136-60. Headboard fabric is Robert Kime's Devonshire Blue.

BLUE HEAVEN

DESIGNER T. KELLER DONOVAN

"I used a lot of this fabric, so the room really holds together."

Chairs, ottoman, head-board, and window seat, all covered in Romo's Leoni in Ice Blue, create serenity through continuity. Curtains and throw pillows are in Zoffany's Maze, and the mirror above the mantel is Donovan's update of an antique convex mirror.

"I think of this blue as 'my blue heaven'—not strong or overpowering. It's a subtle blue."

SPECTACULAR BLUE MOMENTS

Wallpapers

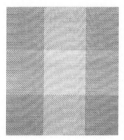

**Check Paperweave
in Aqua from
Schumacher**

**Fig in Blue from
Cole & Son through
Lee Jofa**

**Syrie in Light Blue/
Cream from Studio
Printworks**

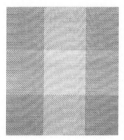

**Clarendon in Color 01
by Osborne & Little**

**Best in Show in Aqua
from Thibaut**

Rose Tarlow's Bamboo wallpaper is the perfect backdrop
for curtains in Chelsea by Rose Tarlow—designed by
ALEX PAPACHRISTIDIS with a custom header that hints
at the shape of a Chinese pagoda.

FRIEZE FRAME

DESIGNER ROBIN BELL

Custom wall color is glazed and combed to give it softness and depth. Bed skirt and club chair are in Hinson's Dottery Blue.

"There's a light charcoal-navy on the stenciled frieze, a dark charcoal-navy outlining the windows, doorways, and base-board, and the walls themselves are glazed a shade I'd call chambray."

"The chair pillow is a vintage damask pillow I found. Its jungle-leaf color is a nice foil for all that blue."

ABOVE: **SMALL WONDER**
DESIGNER: CHAD EISNER
Walls painted Blue Slate 25-21 by Pratt & Lambert enliven this small bedroom.
Pencil Post Bed in walnut from Shelter. The blue print coverlet is from Urban
Outfitters. Curtains are Arts Decoratif by Le Gracieux.

OPPOSITE: **HIP TO BE SQUARE**
DESIGNER: DIAMOND BARATTA
This custom headboard, inspired by blue paint chips, is inset with seven shades
of blue leathers from three different manufacturers. Bedding and curtain fabric is
Kiev from AM Collections.

SHAPELY | DESIGNER: PHOEBE HOWARD

Howard upholstered the curvy headboard in Greystone Home Collection's Walter Ottoman in Slate Blue and covered the low ceiling in a Nina Campbell blue strié wallpaper that looks like wood grain. Walls are painted in Blue Hubbard 8438 by Sherwin-Williams with White Dove trim by Benjamin Moore.

BLUEGRASS | DESIGNER: TOM SCHEERER
Scheerer covered the walls with a Hinson Madagascar cloth, then painted it with
Benjamin Moore Icing on the Cake in high gloss: "Flat paint rarely does it for
me in a new house. I can feel the drywall whimpering through. Grasscloth lends
substance," says Scheerer.

TAILORED

DESIGNER STEVEN GAMBREL

"These are very pale atmospheric blues and greens."

A photograph adds magical ocean blues to the master bedroom. Custom linens from Schweitzer Linen and curtains in Romo's Kenzan pick up on the photo's peaceful, watery shades. Gambrel designed the trim Glover Bed.

DIVINE VISION

DESIGNER

DANA OATLEY ORTEGO

Walls are lime washed in **Larder Blue** by **Portola Paints & Glazes** and the plaster ceiling was left natural for dramatic contrast. The wrought-iron bed was crafted from a salvaged **New Orleans** fence.

"It's spare as a monastery, but the ethereal blue walls transcend any bareness. They're so rich and shadowy, it becomes this sensual, calming, enveloping space."

chapter : 8

BATHROOM BLUES

When you crave a bath de bleu.

LEFT: **"I love the way the blue glass tile adds punch to the master bath." —Robin Bell**

OPPOSITE: **The shine of blue glass tile in this bathroom by Robin Bell is exaggerated against the matte black-and-white river-stone floor; both are from Ann Sacks. A Zoffany print covering a skirted chair adds a shot of fabric for warmth.**

MICHAEL FORMICA GETS MOODY WITH BENJAMIN MOORE CALIFORNIA BLUE 2060-20

"It's a strange color, sort of an old-fashioned blue-print blue. I actually like dark bathrooms with very controlled artificial light. That way you can really hone in on the problems when doing your toilette. Besides, I think dark walls are sexy."

RONALD BRICKE WAKES UP TO PRATT & LAMBERT AUTUMN CROCUS 1141

"Imagine waking up and walking into the brightest, sunniest day. This is a bright lavender blue, moderately intense, very cheerful. It's clean, fresh—guaranteed to perk you up."

MARSHALL WATSON IS TRANSPORTED BY SHERWIN-WILLIAMS GULFSTREAM SW 6768

"Imagine sailing around the Greek islands and looking into the deep teal-blue water. There's a certain sexiness you feel on your skin when you're out on a boat in the sun and the breeze, relaxed and loose. When I walk into a room painted this color, I'm completely transported. Suddenly I'm floating in the Aegean, bobbing up and down with the waves."

WATERCOLOR
DESIGNER: FRANK ROOP
This bathroom gets its airy
look from high ceilings
and walls painted Farrow
& Ball Borrowed Light.
Roop drew the mosaic tile
floor on a computer with
CAD software and **T**ile
Showcase manufactured it
in one piece, like a carpet.

SPECTACULAR BLUE MOMENTS

Wrapping Papers

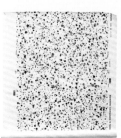

Spatter vinyl-coated paper from **Hinson & Company**

Summer Palace in Blue from **Osborne & Little**

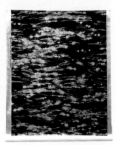

Starglint in Deep Water by **Josh Minnie** for **Flavor Paper**

Solvej in Aqua/Light Blue from **Sandberg** through **Stark Wallcovering**

Beadazzled Leaf in Aqua from **Maya Romanoff**

This powder room was plain and forgettable until **KRISTEN PANITCH** gave it personality with **Cole & Son's Orchid.**

ABOVE: **SILVER LINING**
DESIGNER: PAOLO MOSCHINO
"There's a powdery blue on the walls—Farrow & Ball Light Blue—and a
powdery gray—Farrow & Ball Old White—on the wainscoting. Very soft.
When you walk in every morning, you don't want to have a shock. It's a
soothing combination," says Moschino.

OPPOSITE: **GREAT COVER-UP**
DESIGNER: T. KELLER DONOVAN
Donovan picked a blue indoor/outdoor fabric—Clarence House's Outdoor
Coral in Marine—and went all out with it, upholstering walls and a stool.

SPECTACULAR BLUE MOMENTS

Building Blocks

**Abalone from
Domani Tile**

**Bubbles by Alluvial
Realm Tile**

**Mediterranean Oasis
from Casa Ceramica**

**Blue Sky
by Art FX**

**Vanilla Swirl from
Casa Cielo Tile**

**Peacock by Anima
Ceramic Design**

**Crossings Florenz
from Country Floors**

In this bathroom by **CATHY KINCAID**, Farrow & Ball
Old White paint on the walls has the same muted tone as
Moroccan Cross and Star tiles by Ann Sacks.

A SANCTUARY

DESIGNER BONESTEEL
TROUT HALL

"Everything in
the room is sort
of floating. The
vanities and
the tub are off
the floor."

"The turquoise blue tile is like the ocean just outside. And it's streaked with a little bit of white, which gives it a ripple."

A watery frieze of blue glass tiles wraps the room and unifies the separate areas. Repose 1-by-6-inch tiles in Splash by Waterworks. The Zen bath by Lefroy Brooks floats on wood blocks like a piece of sculpture.

chapter : 9

FRESH AIR BLUES

When even a cloudless sky isn't enough blue for you.

LEFT: **Blue cushions on deck chairs in an outdoor space by Jodi Macklin look shipshape against the crisp white portico.**

OPPOSITE: **"We carried the nautical theme to the pool-house with life preservers and curtains with rope tiebacks and rods threaded through chunky grommets."** —Jodi Macklin

EASY DOES IT
DESIGNER: T. KELLER DONOVAN
On a Miami high-rise terrace,
banquette and pillows in
Perennials' White Ishi are
trimmed in blue and white
Bikini and mixed with blue
plastic stools from Lebello—
a simple way to make a
cookie-cutter space unique.

SOUTHWESTERN STYLE | DESIGNER: CATHY KINCAID
An Arizona loggia's furniture is upholstered in a glowing blue fabric from Perennials. "It's durable and so pretty you could use it in a living room," says Kincaid.

AMERICAN IDYLL

DESIGNER MICHAEL SMITH

"There's no rule other than the divine factor: What's going to look divine?"

There's no reason why outdoor furniture shouldn't be as comfortable as indoor. The inviting daybeds on this upstairs balcony are by **JANUS et Cie** and are covered in outdoor fabric from **Kravet**. The starry print on two of the pillows is Smith's Star Atlantico in Ocean, from **Jasper**.

SPECTACULAR BLUE MOMENTS

Muscle Relaxers

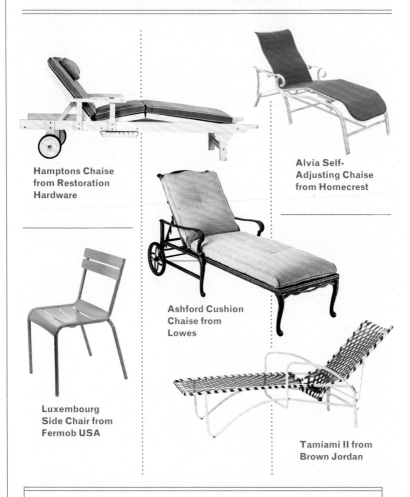

Hamptons Chaise from Restoration Hardware

Alvia Self-Adjusting Chaise from Homecrest

Ashford Cushion Chaise from Lowes

Luxembourg Side Chair from Fermob USA

Tamiami II from Brown Jordan

Lounge chairs from Smith & Hawkin topped with throws from Yarnz create a cozy spot for afternoon napping.

Part 2

What works with blue?
Designers always seem to know what
hues will live together in harmony.
Here they show you how they do it.

Walls painted a
pale blue, Benjamin
Moore Clear Skies,
take the edge off all
the super-vibrant
tones in a room by
JOHN WILLEY.

chapter : 10

BLUE & WHITE

Clean, crisp and never out of style.

ABOVE: "I edit things down to the basics and then let the curtains and accessories be the icing on the cupcake." —T. Keller Donovan

OPPOSITE: Chairs and sofa, upholstered in Romo's Linara, rest on a blue plaid rug—grounding the room in vivid blue. Curtains are in Peter Fasano's Dotty and throw pillows are in Peter Fasano's Camp Leaves.

LOUD AND CLEAR

DESIGNER
LYNN MORGAN

- **T**ightly upholstered sofas in **C**owtan & Tout's **F**lorian Plain in dark blue are a strong tailored foundation.

- **C**risp white piping adds polish.

- **N**atural texture: Rattan end tables, bamboo window shades and wicker armchairs warm up all the cool blue.

- **T**hrow pillows in China Seas' Zig Zag and Sea-Cloth's Gypsy in Bloom are welcome shots of modernity.

PLAINSPOKEN YANKEE

DESIGNER
TOM SCHEERER

- With its blue and white palette and unfussy furniture, this room embraces the beauty of simplicity.

- Hits of bright blue, like the icy hues in the striped rug, are dramatic against walls painted **Benjamin Moore Atrium White.**

- Floral throw pillows in **Kathryn M. Ireland's Floral Batik** soften large rectilinear sofas.

- Traditional blue windowpane fabric, **Samba in Bleu Matelot from Pierre Frey,** looks ultra modern on a traditional armchair.

ABOVE: **SHIPSHAPE**
DESIGNER: PHOEBE HOWARD
In this living room symmetry prevails. "Furniture in strong colors makes strong silhouettes, so you want it to look orderly," says Howard. The club chairs and sofa, both in Sapphire from Thomas Dare, dominate the room, and grasscloth walls lend a cozy feeling.

. . . .

OPPOSITE: **WOODSY**
DESIGNERS: KIM COLEMAN & MICHELE GREEN
Cedar-plank walls, shells, a driftwood chandelier, and lots of blue give this room both a woodsy and a beachy chic. Shell artwork from Palecek. Chandelier from Mecox. Sofa pillows from Restoration Hardware. Wisteria rug. William-Wayne artichoke lamp.

ON THE GRID

DESIGNER
MEG BRAFF

- Intricate Chinese
  Lattice wallpaper from
  Bob Collins sets the tone:
  a fun, 1950s resort look.

- Echoing the wallpaper's
  colors and lines is a blue-
  and-white pillow from
  Williams-Sonoma Home.

- Scalamandré sofa in a
  solid, Hinson's Pantigo
  Cloth in Blue, calms
  the pattern.

- Round white side tables
  from Chelsea House
  mimic the circles in the
  wallpaper, and brass
  floor lamps from Visual
  Comfort add shine.

BEACH HOUSE BLUES | DESIGNER: MARSHALL WATSON
A blue backsplash, Veneto glass tiles from Stone Source, takes over
one whole wall. "It's the one big, bold stroke of color, but boy, is it big,"
says Watson.

MAPPED OUT | **DESIGNERS: KIM COLEMAN & MICHELE GREEN**

Artist Lori Barnaby painted a nautical chart on walls. "In keeping with the theme," says Coleman, "the blues of the sofa, chairs, rug, and accessories create an aquatic aura." Dash & Albert Diamond Denim rug. Ankasa pillows. An antique library chair is covered in Edelman leather.

CLEAN LIVING

DESIGNER
D A V I D   K L E I N B E R G

- "We used carefully placed punches of blue," says Kleinberg. "Bursts of color have so much impact."

- Pale aqua colors maximize light and speak quietly.

- Curtains in Julienne Taffeta Stripe from Brunschwig & Fils convey an elegant modernity, the perfect backdrop for a 1930s English oak table and vintage Paul Hanson lamp.

- The fabric headboard and bed skirt, covered in Montague in Sky from Rose Tarlow, seem to float above the floor, adding to the restful vibe.

BEDTIME STORY

DESIGNER
TOM STRINGER

- Twin iron beds are painted navy blue as a strong contrast to walls painted Benjamin Moore White Dove.

- Floral duvets from Anthropologie soften the stark lines of the furniture.

- The lines of wide stripes in pillow shams and bed skirts from Pottery Barn work well with the duvets' overblown curvy pattern.

- Blue curtains have a dental-molding edge that echoes the pillow shams' stripes.

chapter : 11

BLUE & YELLOW

Classic, sunny and happy.

LEFT: "I think it's exciting because it has this kind of casual elegance. It's very light and colorful."
—Albert Hadley

OPPOSITE: Surprising hits of bright yellow on benches provide youthful energy against cool, refined shades of blue in this living room by Albert Hadley.

NOT MELLOW YELLOW

DESIGNER
JONATHAN ADLER

- "The programmatic choice would have been to do the chairs in turquoise. But if we'd done that, the room would have looked impersonal. Instead we threw in the wild card of lemon yellow," says Adler.

- Vibrant Chinese Chippendale chairs around a modern Warren Platner table are festive, electric touches.

- Simple eye-catching blocks of turquoise curtains, in Hinson's Montauk Texture in Aegean, keep the rug's pattern in check.

GALLIC AMERICAN
DESIGNER: ALESSANDRA BRANCA
Pale yellow walls and a Pierre Frey
print on chairs create a wonderfully
French feeling in this breakfast
area. The banquette wears a
Cowtan & Tout stripe.

POP STAR | DESIGNER: JOE NYE
A cool blue table skirt, in Claremont's Semis Montrichard, calms down the
intensity of hot pink chairs and bright yellow walls in Yellowhammer GH100
by Ralph Lauren Paint.

WHITE STRIPS

DESIGNER
TOM STRINGER

- The four-poster bed's headboard, in Ralph Lauren's Coastal Stripe in Yellow & White, is the room's showstopper.

- Stools are painted bright white and upholstered in Raoul Textiles' Chunari in Blue Willow for dramatic contrast.

- Walls and ceiling are painted Benjamin Moore White Dove and the chandelier, which has hung in this spot for decades, got a coat of fresh white paint.

- Yellow bedside tables, Jacqui from Bungalow 5, add another splash of sunshine.

BLUE & BROWN

Warm, earthy and oh-so rich!

LEFT: **"The chairs are tufted in pannéed leather that's been treated with a slight pearlescence. There's flat-out glamour happening and they certainly add horsepower, don't you think?"**
—Jeffrey Bilhuber

OPPOSITE: **Jeffrey Bilhuber** upholstered chairs in **Edelman Luster Leather** in **Pond** and covered their backs with **Chappas Textiles' Bodem.** The dining room was treated to fourteen coats of brown lacquer for maximum luster.

A SEPARATE PEACE

DESIGNER
ALEX PAPACHRISTIDIS

- "We needed to give the family room its own identity to separate it from the open kitchen, so we painted the walls dark brown," says Papachristidis.

- Cushions on the cane chairs, in Jasper's Tree of Life, unify all the deep blues and browns in the room.

- The geometric rug by Beauvais Carpets defines the shape of the room and lends a youthful vibe to a traditional space.

ABOVE: **NATURAL INSTINCTS**
DESIGNER: ROBERT STILIN
The icy blues of the throw pillows—a Classic Cloth stripe and a
Clarence House solid—are magnified and enhanced by all the
natural brown hues surrounding them.

....

OPPOSITE: **AGING GRACEFULLY**
**DESIGNER: BABS WATKINS, JULIE WATKINS BAKER, &
ELEANOR CUMMINGS**
Moody blues on gently worn surfaces—like Louis XV carved
walnut front doors and a gilt-edged Venetian lantern—mix with
browns and silvery grays to impart soul, grace, and history.

NEW WAVE TRADITIONAL

DESIGNER
SCOTT SANDERS

- A Wedgwood blue and chocolate brown palette warms this new construction.

- All the colors came out of the wingchair's paisley upholstery—Scalamandré's Dromoland in Sky Blue.

- Accessories like blue and white ginger jars fit the vernacular of a traditional, settled country house.

- A blue lampshade on a table lamp and blue candles add mood to evening light.

- The sofa's timeless shape upholstered in an earthy camel color lends the place a cozy familiarity, like it's been lived in a long time.

TROPICAL PARADISE

DESIGNER
TOM SCHEERER

- **Walls in Benjamin Moore Marine Blue** provide an arresting backdrop for an exotic fabric headboard, upholstered in **New Batik** from **China Seas**.

- The secret to the drama is the mix of deep blues and chocolate browns with the whitest whites, along with the delightful play of scale among the prints.

- Even swing-arm sconces silhouette dramatically in crisp lines against sumptuous blue walls.

BLUE & GREEN

Fresh and youthful, with a nature vibe.

ABOVE: **A collection of antique blue glass in an entry by John Willey pops against walls painted Benjamin Moore Fresh Cut Grass 2026-50.**

OPPOSITE: **"The chandelier is so dramatic when you come in at night. It has this extraordinary shadow effect—a cluster of round shadows like bubbles appear all around the blue stairwell. You feel like you're underwater." —John Willey**

WILD CIVILITY

DESIGNER
STEVEN GAMBREL

- Walls are painted in two vivid **Benjamin Moore** colors—**Cedar Green** and **Marlboro Blue**—for an effect that's as offbeat as it friendly.

- "It's easier for me to use colors like these when they're framed," says Gambrel about the way the moldings frame the wall color. "With a raised panel detail you can use a brighter color because it's broken up by white— it's framed like a painting, not bleeding into infinity. It gives a punchier, crisp edge to the room."

- Gambrel's blue **Stanton Club chair**, with rect-angles of contrasting green welting, echoes the bookcase's boxy grid.

COLORFUL PUNCH
DESIGNER: ASHLEY WHITTAKER
In a breakfast area, Windsor chairs with citrus-green cushions are piped in blue, while the blue banquette cushion has green piping. Walls papered in Baldwin Bamboo by Scalamandré unify the theme.

FLAT-OUT CHIC | DESIGNER: HEALING BARSANTI
A kitchen banquette, in Sari Majolica by Raoul Textiles, injects a big dose of
bright blue, which looks great with the more subdued olive leather on the chairs.
Walls are Brilliant White with trim in White Dove, both Benjamin Moore.

MORNING EDITION

- "I like bedrooms to be fresh, not dark cocoons," says Morgan—and what could be fresher than the combination of sky blue and apple green?

- The bed, upholstered in Early Spring in Sky from Victoria Hagan, has a clean-lined aesthetic that's tempered by the worn patina of the bedside dressers.

- The chaise, in Pierre Frey's Shabby in Absinthe, is trimmed with white piping for a neat, tailored look.

- A cashmere throw brings the apple-green color up onto the bed.

BLUE & ORANGE

Hot, tropical and daring.

LEFT: **"The room reminds me of 1960s Howard Johnson's colors—that wonderfully intense orange and aqua blue—but modernized a bit. It's such a terrific vintage palette."** —John Willey

OPPOSITE: **For this guest room, John Willey chose China Seas' Lysette Reverse Orange for curtains and bed pillows. The orange isn't too bright because it's printed on tan linen rather than cotton.**

chapter : 14 :

PERFECT HARMONY

DESIGNER
BROCKSCHMIDT
& COLEMAN

- "We didn't vary the colors much to keep things calm," says Coleman.

- Colors are restricted to pale blues and coral, with bits of white for crispness.

- The designers relied on symmetry to help the room feel comfortable, in keeping with their credo: Balance creates harmony.

- Walls painted a watery greenish blue from Farrow & Ball, Teresa's Green 236, are a soft foil for hot corals.

- Grass yoga mats framed inside blue panel moldings keep formality at bay.

LUXURY HOUSES COUNTRY

BRIGHT STAR | DESIGNER: ASHLEY WHITTAKER
Turquoise on tinted linen from Quadrille on walls, and chairs dressed in coral
linen from Travers—together they lighten the feel of the formal mahogany table.

EASY AND OPEN | DESIGNER: ANN WOLF

Tangerine and blue upholstered chairs surrounding a Christian Liaigre table keep the mood casual.

ABOVE: **NAP TIME**
DESIGNER: ALLISON CACCOMA
High-gloss blue walls in Benjamin Moore Harbor Haze 2136-60, an
antique chaise, and big coral pillows make a cozy spot for a nap in
this master bedroom.

OPPOSITE: **MAXIMALISM**
DESIGNER: JONATHAN BERGER
Berger designed the mirrored bed after a 1940s Serge Roche piece
and lined it in Agnes in Salt Air from Silk Trading Company for even
more drama.

chapter : 15

BLUE & BEIGE

Polished, chic and super-glam.

LEFT: **Jay Jeffers painted a pool house in all-over blue stripes, for a tent-like feeling, and then hung antique glass pendants from the apex of the ceiling.**

OPPOSITE: **"This was an area where I decided to go a little bit crazy—where people are going to walk in and go, 'Wow! I love it!'"**
—Jay Jeffers

ABOVE: **HOMEY INSTINCT**
DESIGNER: KRISTEN PANITCH
The bold pattern and neutral colors of Cole & Son's Mimosa wallpaper against the blue sofa, covered in Mali Stripe by Jasper, adds
"a sense of daring and quiet at the same time," says Panitch.

OPPOSITE: **REGAL MANNER**
DESIGNER: TOBI FAIRLEY
Blue begins in the foyer here. Opal blue Venetian glass lamps from
Swank Lighting hold their own against a glam overblown damask
pattern on walls, Veneziano wallpaper by Nina Campbell.

COUP DE BLEU

DESIGNER
MEG BRAFF

- "The printed fabric in the guest bedroom is whimsical," Braff says, "but the beige and aqua palette is very restful."

- The lively bed and curtain fabric, China Seas' Lyford Background, works with wide-striped wallpaper, First Editions' Millennium Stripe, because both are large-scale patterns.

- Shots of frosty blue, like these Jonathan Adler ottomans, add sophistication and polish to all the neutral tones.

IT'S CURTAINS

DESIGNER
JEFFREY BILHUBER

- Curtains between rooms—
  these are in Cameo in
  Robin's Egg from AM
  Collections—are a favorite
  Bilhuber device, used to
  pull a thread of color (like
  blue) through a house.

- In the living room (fore-
  ground), the pair of armchairs are covered in the
  same blue fabric as the
  curtains, so the mood is
  elegant, not busy.

- Ralph Lauren's chunky
  woven-rush Joshua Tree
  armchairs at each end
  of the dining table and a
  pair of French oak and
  rush fauteuils in the living
  room add natural texture,
  balancing all the fabric.

chapter 16

BLUE & RED

Dynamic, noble, and dignified.

LEFT: **Christopher Maya upholstered walls in Holland & Sherry's Militaire worsted wool in Indigo for heightened drama.**

OPPOSITE: **"The blue becomes bluer when you see red against it, and the red becomes redder."** **—Christopher Maya**

LIVING COLOR | DESIGNER: SHAZALYNN CAVIN-WINFREY
Sky blue walls, painted Valspar's 7005-2 Stillness, pair beautifully with lively
striped chairs and draperies. "The color gives this sitting room the most natural,
vibrant light," says Cavin-Winfrey.

OTTOMAN RULES
DESIGNER: TOBI FAIRLEY
Aqua and red are a powerful combination when all the other colors are neutral. The ottoman is covered in Eliana from William Yeoward.

RICH AND HANDSOME

DESIGNER
CHRISTOPHER MAYA

- **White walls and a robin's egg blue rug from Elizabeth Eakins are the perfect cool backdrops for pops of hot Crayola red.**

- **To create architectural interest where there was none, the bar was given a slick coat of Benjamin Moore Black Panther, then painted with Benjamin Moore Heritage Red.**

- **Red armchairs upholstered in Clarence House Belgian Linen and red trim on the antique French chairs lend the room unexpected attitude.**

ABOVE: **PILLOW TALK**
DESIGNER: KRISTIN HEIN & PHILIP COZZI
The red, white, and blue palette in this beach-house bedroom
is punctuated by chrome accents that suggest a yacht's
below decks. The headboard, in Big Island from Donghia,
is a riff on waves.

....

OPPOSITE: **SHABBY CHIC INDUSTRIAL**
DESIGNER: AMY NEUNSINGER
To play off the Chinese red of the beams, Benjamin Moore
Million Dollar Red, Neunsinger painted the walls turquoise—
Benjamin Moore Jade Garden.

Part 3

How blue are you?
Designers take you from the palest
blues to the boldest bravest hues.

Designer **MOISES ESQUENAZI** painted his **Los Angeles** house blue, then decided to do his front door in a punchy orange to be "chic and dramatic."

chapter : 17

THE BASHFUL BLUES

Sky, Aqua, Powder, Misty…

LEFT: **"It's the epitome of Hollywood glam. The silk satin headboard sets the tone. Then you throw in the layers of misty blues, the lustrous bedding, the mirrored furniture and you're so far down the road you can't go back."** —**Tobi Fairley**

OPPOSITE: **"I just love this Barbara Barry wallpaper,"** Fairley says about **Chic Link in Seamist from Kravet.** **"The print is so small and subtle, like a man's tie pattern."** Baker's **Paris** bed is dressed in **Ann Gish's** quilted **Frost Charmeuse** coverlet and shams.

LIGHT SHOW

DESIGNER
KIM COLEMAN

- For this coastal location, Kim Coleman chose a soothing watery blue-green—Farrow & Ball Powder Blue 23—for walls.

- To heighten the impact of the wall color, sofa and loveseats are upholstered in white— Scalamandré's Harper Matelassé.

- Curtains hang on white-painted rods, and stripes echo the blue-green on the walls, keeping the feeling cool, calm, and collected.

" I've always been drawn to blue. It's a heavenly color to live with. I've never seen a blue I don't like. "

"This is a comfortable, restful, generous room, designed for entertaining on a big or small scale."

"So far I have never, ever regretted a blue that I've used."

SPECTACULAR BLUE MOMENTS

Fairest of Them All

Classic Mohair in White Caps from J. Robert Scott

Aripeka in Hydrangea from Rogers & Goffigon

Striate in Aqua from Kate Gabriel through Studio Four NYC

Wolfe in Cloud from Theo

Fiori in Atlantic City on Sea Mist from Rose Tarlow Melrose Place

Wool Sateen in Blue Smoke from Beacon Hill

Atmosphere in Marina from Nomi Fabrics

Cloque de Coton in Color 8 from Dominique Kieffer by Rubelli

VICENTE WOLF used a subtle blue upholstered ottoman and pale blue throw pillows to add drama, but not too much drama, to a peaceful minimal palette.

ENGLISH LESSON

DESIGNER
ASHLEY WHITTAKER

- There are lots of different patterns in this bedroom, but none are jarring because colors are restricted to washed-out blues and creams.

- The wallpaper, by **N**ina **C**ampbell through **O**sborne & **L**ittle, has a lot of movement but it stays in the background because colors are muted.

- Creamy white window shades are trimmed in the same blue plaid that covers the ottoman, and the vanity table skirt is in the same **C**owtan & **T**out floral as the bolster, so the room feels balanced and peaceful.

"**The white linen sofa and dressing table with the white shell mirror add to the overall serenity of the bedroom.**"

"I love the blues and warm creams of this master bedroom. And I made sure the husband had a comfortable chaise to sit in on Sundays, to read the paper, and take a nap."

ISLAND LIFE

VOGUE FASHION

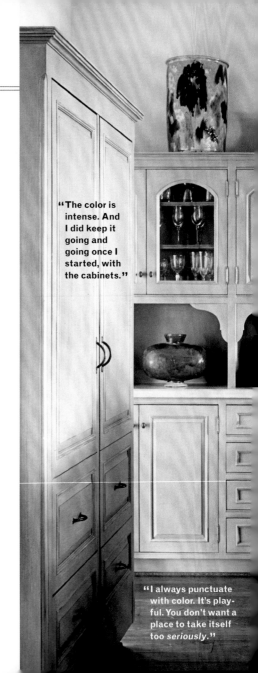

COOKING WITH BLUE

DESIGNER
CHRISTINA ROTTMAN

- A blackened umber glaze was applied to the cabinets, then painted over with a turquoise glaze to intensify the sky-blue hue.

- Intricate moldings, backsplashes, even baseboards are painted blue, for the most luxurious feel possible.

- Buffing, stippling, and scraping give the cabinets a timeworn look and soften the impact of their sheen.

- Limestone countertops are creamy and matte, a visual relief from the full-on color.

"The color is intense. And I did keep it going and going once I started, with the cabinets."

"I always punctuate with color. It's playful. You don't want a place to take itself too *seriously.*"

"I wanted this jolt of color to emphasize that the kitchen is the joyful heart of the house."

"This kitchen is the right scale—you don't want strong color in the biggest room."

FASHION STATEMENT

DESIGNER
KIM COLEMAN

- Symmetry and a restricted color palette, just black and white with turquoise, keeps things restful.

- Turquoise stripes around the perimeter of the room have a clean geometric feeling that's repeated in the **Oly** bed, the **Devon-shire** mirror, and the **Frette** bedding.

- The **Oly** armchair, covered in **Teddy** in **Turquoise** from **Design-Tex**, moves turquoise to the opposite side of the room for balance.

"Since I was a child I've always been drawn to blue."

"My two favorite words are 'Trust me.' And they did. And you know what? Everybody loves this room."

"Turquoise with the black and white adds an element of surprise to the guest room."

SPECTACULAR BLUE MOMENTS

Middle Ground

Tile Leaf in Slate from SeaCloth at Lee Jofa

Peonies in Aqua by Christopher Farr Cloth through Thomas Lavin

Bang Na in Royal Blue from Jim Thompson

Gastaad Plaid in Capri by Eric Cohler for Lee Jofa

Las Palmas Damask in Wedgwood by Nancy Corzine

Jupon Bouquet in Azure Blue and Warm White from Fortuny

Somerset Linen in Sky from Cowtan & Tout

Baroda II in Indigo on Natural from Lisa Fine Textiles

> With the help of gray-blue chairs slipcovered in Kathryn M. Ireland's Gitana and a roman shade in Olona from AM Collections, **MILLY DE CABROL** creates the ultimate serenity.

ZEN DEN

DESIGNER
TOBI FAIRLEY

- Because of the lack of contrast, periwinkle blue becomes almost a neutral.

- Venetian plaster walls, tinted Sherwin-Williams Silvermist, capture light, so the room feels airy in spite of all the color.

- Baker's Neue sofa is softened with shaggy Calypso pillows.

- The rug from Tamarian is a necessary shot of pattern.

"The client wanted to bring home some of the beauty she'd seen at resorts and spas . . . serene, sophisticated glamour."

"The painting over the sofa is almost an extension of the wall, but a little grayer."

"I wanted to wrap the living room in layers of pale blue tones without a lot of contrast."

BEDTIME STORY

DESIGNER
SCOTT SANDERS

- The blue-green tone of the walls is perfect for brightening dark mahogany.

- Because Zoffany's Broccatello Ciniglia—the fabric on the bench—inspired the room's entire palette, there's nothing jarring. It's peaceful.

- Walls painted Benjamin Moore Spring in Aspen are cheerful in the day and cocoon like at night.

- A small blue-and-white needlepoint rug defines the sitting area.

"I love blue. There's often a blue filter over everything in my dreams."

"I stick to one blue, and just move it up or down a shade or two."

"This green-blue is a great color for warming up new houses and cozying up big rooms."

chapter 19

THE BOLD, BRAVE SHADES

Navy, Indigo, Cobalt, Midnight,
Dark Turquoise…

LEFT: "I just wanted to be happy—and color makes you happy. Turquoise is intense and exciting."
—Bunny Williams

OPPOSITE: The red egg chair's curves glow against walls painted Benjamin Moore California Breeze, a blue echoed in the Quadrille Veneto fronts and seats of the armchairs.

HAUTE VOLTAGE

DESIGNER
JAMIE DRAKE

- Holly Hunt wallcovering is handwoven yarn-dyed raffia but reads from even a short distance as denim.

- The predominant blue is indigo so there aren't lots of different blues battling for superiority.

- The bed is covered in two emphatic Bergamo prints—Hyde Park for the seat and Rosegarten for the cushions—and it's topped with throw pillows in Schumacher's Zenyatta Mondatta.

- A lime-green chair, covered in Pierre Frey's Palmarola, is another jolt of energy.

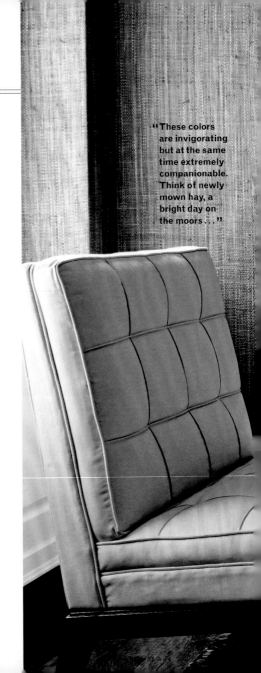

"These colors are invigorating but at the same time extremely companionable. Think of newly mown hay, a bright day on the moors..."

"It started with the throw pillows. They're a 2008 interpretation of a 1960s version of a classic 18th-century flame stitch."

"Most people aren't fearless enough. The reason there are so many bland interiors is that people are scared."

AMERICAN BEAUTY

DESIGNER
T. KELLER DONOVAN

- Peter Fasano's Sarum Strié paper feels crisp and fresh by day and deep and sensuous by night.

- Two small pewter chandeliers keep the mood casual and make a virtue of necessity: "One big one would have hung mid-mirror," Donovan says. Their silver color is echoed in nailhead trim on the chairs.

- Instead of using real blue plates, Donovan enlarged prints of Staffordshire plates.

- The camel color of the carpet, Stark's Ruad Squares, keeps dark blue from overpowering the room.

- Updated Queen Anne mirror from William Switzer pulls light onto dark walls.

"My client loves blue so much she wanted a completely blue house."

"I like to do small dressmaker details—like that tiny blue line around the lamp shades and the pictures—that echo in things like the white picot ribbon on the chairs and the carpet bindings."

"That's not blue paint—it's strié paper. I have a phobia about faux painting!"

SPECTACULAR BLUE MOMENTS

Power Blues

Thick as Thieves in Dark Blue from Holly Hunt

La Garoupe in Indigo from Ralph Lauren Home

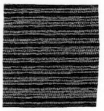

Well Rounded in Tide from Designtex

Luce in Navy from Madeline Weinrib

20953 in Indigo from Duralee

St. Tropez in Pool from Schumacher

Velours Aspen in Bleu Navy from Pierre Frey

Hanoi in Ben Hal Blue from Donghia

The blue ikat fabric on the sofa, Adras in Blue from Lee Industries, lends this room its strong personality. "I did what most people wouldn't do. I took the busiest fabric and put it on the biggest piece, the sofa," says editor in chief **NEWELL TURNER**.

BLUES CLUB

DESIGNER
MEG BRAFF

- The sofas, upholstered in Hinson's Rawlston in Dunham Blue, bring the deep blue color down into the room so that it isn't top-heavy.

- "One day I arrived, and my client had just purchased that gorgeous lime-green lamp. I thought, 'That's brilliant. Let's go with it and repeat the color somewhere.' So we upholstered the ottoman in lime green leather, and added a little tape trim to the other lampshades to echo that," says Braff.

- Roman shades in Abaco stripe by China Seas introduce a bit of modern hip to the room's traditional elements.

"Blue also works well off of so many colors. Even though the house is strong on color, it still feels neutral, because there's also a good dose of white balancing it all. White cuts through and allows the whole to breathe."

"Because the clients had four young children, durability in the family room was key. The dark blue fabric on the sofas, the leather ottoman, and the sisal rug are all practically bulletproof."

"Grasscloth is great for giving a little warmth and character and weight to a new house, a feeling of 'It's always been here.' It's nice to have that layer, but still have it feel fresh and clean."

"I'm a blue person. There's hardly a blue I don't like. When I get a client who's also a blue person, there is going to be a lot of blue"

CITY SLICKER

- Lacquered walls are in Farrow & Ball Hague Blue. "It doesn't look dark so much as rich," says Redd.

- Herringbone wood floors, left bare, add subtle pattern to the room's big blocks of saturated color.

- Maison Jansen slipper chairs are upholstered in Velours de Soie Uni in Bleu de France from Prelle. "It's a divine fabric, with an inky, lustrous quality," says Redd.

- The sumptuous sofa, dressed in Opera in Cedar from Holland & Sherry, softens the walls' sleek blue glow.

"This apartment is used more heavily in the winter, so the palette is wintry. It's all about freezing-cold martinis and chicken potpies, comfort and coziness."

"The sofa from Lucca & Co is in loden green silk velvet. I love all colors, but I really love jewel tones."

"Walls are lacquered, which is a great way to do a dark, moody color because the reflective surface has the quality of light in a Vermeer painting. I'm a huge fan of lacquered walls. It's expensive, but beautiful and quite durable."

"The low Louis XV– style slipper chairs have peacock blue silk velvet, which isn't exactly the color of the walls but works with them in an offbeat way."

: PHOTO CREDITS :

Copyright © 2011 by Hearst Communications, Inc.

Book design by Nancy Leonard

Library of Congress Cataloging-in-Publication Data

Cregan, Lisa.
  House beautiful : blue / Lisa Cregan.
      p. cm.
  ISBN 978-1-58816-823-8
  1. Blue in interior decoration. I. House beautiful. II. Title. III. Title: Blue.
  NK2115.5.C6C74 2010
  747'.94–dc22

                            2010008322

10 9 8 7 6 5 4 3 2 1

Published by Hearst Books
A Division of Sterling Publishing Co., Inc.
387 Park Avenue South, New York, NY 10016

House Beautiful is a registered trademark of Hearst Communications, Inc.

www.housebeautiful.com

For information about custom editions, special sales, premium and corporate
purchases, please contact Sterling Special Sales Department at 800-805-5489
or specialsales@sterlingpublishing.com.

Distributed in Canada by Sterling Publishing
c/o Canadian Manda Group, 165 Dufferin Street
Toronto, Ontario, Canada M6K 3H6

Distributed in Australia by Capricorn Link (Australia) Pty. Ltd.
P.O. Box 704, Windsor, NSW 2756 Australia

Manufactured in China

Sterling ISBN 978-1-58816-823-8

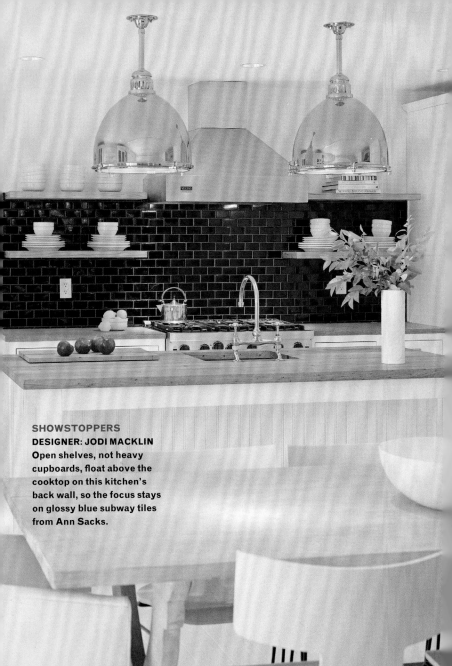

SHOWSTOPPERS
DESIGNER: JODI MACKLIN
Open shelves, not heavy
cupboards, float above the
cooktop on this kitchen's
back wall, so the focus stays
on glossy blue subway tiles
from Ann Sacks.